FINDING YOU

How to Live the Life You Love
A self discovery book

BONITA A. BENSON

Finding You "How to Live the Life You Love"
By Bonita A. Benson

Cover Illustrated by Bonita A. Benson
Cover Created by Jazzy Kitty Publications
Logo Designs by Andre M. Saunders/Jess Zimmerman
Editor: Anelda L. Attaway

© 2021 Bonita A. Benson
ISBN 978-1-954425-39-2
Library of Congress Control Number: 2021925920

All rights reserved. This book is protected by the copyright laws of the United States of America. This book may not be copied or reprinted for commercial gain or profit. The use of short quotations or occasional page copying for personal or group study is permitted and encouraged. Permission will be granted upon request. This book is for Worldwide Distribution and printed in the United States of America, published by Jazzy Kitty Publications utilizing Microsoft Publishing Software.

DEDICATIONS

This book is dedicated to my heroes; my dad and brother, Edmund Benson Sr. and Edmund Benson Jr., who are with the Lord. You've always been the wind beneath my wings. Also, to my dear Mother, Rebecca Benson, who is my super cheerleader and has always believed in me.

ACKNOWLEDGMENTS

First giving honor and praise to my Lord and Savior Jesus Christ. Thank you, Heavenly Father, for unconditional love, unfailing favor and all the many blessings bestowed upon me. Thank you for the Holy Spirit's guidance in the manifestation of my dreams.

Thank you, Vincent and Desya, my precious children, for allowing me to fulfill God's will for my life. Your presence in my life is the force that motivated me to face my fears, believe in myself and live the life I love.

Thank you to my parents, who provided me with an amazing childhood. Words cannot express my gratitude for my mother, Rebecca Benson, who stood by me and supported my dreams every step of the way. My father, Edmund Benson Sr., who challenged me to greater heights and has been a large part of my success.

To my three siblings, Mary Acree and George W. Acree III, you are precious to me. Thank you for challenging me to find my voice and walk in my own greatness. Edmund Benson Jr., you were and always will be my heartbeat.

Finally, I cannot express my gratitude for the wisdom and mentoring I have received from the most profound professors, women, and preachers of the 20th and 21st century. You have stimulated greatness in my life. Also, I appreciate "the sisterhood" for toiling with me; proofreading, encouraging, and supporting me. God has blessed my life with your friendships.

TABLE OF CONTENTS

INTRODUCTION i
CHAPTER ONE: CLEAR OUT ALL AREAS OF DOUBT 02
    Shedding Your Doubt 02
    Self-Doubt 03
    Critical Self-Talk 04
    Doubting Relationships 05
CHAPTER TWO: AVOID OVERTHINKING 10
    Letting Go of the Past 10
    How to Let Go of Regret 11
    That Little Nagging Voice 12
    Social Anxiety 13
    Getting Over Overthinking 15
CHAPTER THREE: EXPLORE YOUR COMMUNITY 17
    Jump In 17
    Be Authentic 19
    Let Go of Expectations 21
    Let Go of Perfection 22
    Let Go of the Worst-Case Scenario 23
    Focus on the Moment 24
CHAPTER FOUR: PRACTICE MINDFULNESS 26
    Mindfulness 27
    Mindfulness and Self-Compassion 29
    Constantly Compassionate 30
CHAPTER FIVE: LET GO OF WHAT HOLDS YOU BACK 33

    Let Go of Resentment..33
    Let Go of Fear 34
    Let Go of Negative People 35
    How to Set Boundaries...37
    Allow Yourself to Let Go 38
CHAPTER SIX: HOLD ON TO WHAT MOVES YOU FORWARD 40
    Clarify Your Values 40
    Goal Setting..41
    Explore Spirituality 42
    Embrace Your Greatness 44
SUMMARY 47
AFFIRMATION REFLECTIONS...52
15 SELF-DISCOVERY QUESTIONS 116
ABOUT THE AUTHOR 119

"Chasing a person doesn't give you value or build values in you. You earn your value by chasing morality and practicing dignity."

- SHANNON L. ALDER

INTRODUCTION

Creating the life you want to live is perfectly within your reach! By truly embracing yourself, you're able to embrace life with excitement and gratitude. Do you need more self-compassion? How can you increase positivity in all areas of your life?

There are 6 actions you can apply to your life that will increase your feelings of self-love and self-worth:

- **Chapter #1**: **Clear Out All Areas of Doubt.** In this chapter, we will look at the various areas in your life where you may harbor doubts. With this knowledge, you can begin the process of letting go of these doubts.
- **Chapter #2**: **Avoid Overthinking.** In this chapter, we will discuss the various ways in which our minds speed so far ahead of us. You can now let go of regret, of the nagging voice in the back of your head, and of fear of social situations.
- **Chapter #3**: **Explore Your Community.** This chapter covers the importance of building a solid community. The best place to start is exactly where you are. You can now go out into your community and engage with others on a new and authentic level.
- **Chapter #4**: **Practice Mindfulness.** Declutter your mind by getting centered in the present moment. This chapter provides techniques for coming back to the present moment and having compassion for yourself there.
- **Chapter #5**: **Let Go of What Holds You Back.** In order to

move forward, you must let go fully of the things that no longer help you grow. Let go of your anger, fear, and the people who keep you from your fullest potential.

- **Chapter #6: Hold Onto What Moves You Forward.** Get clear with your values and use them to set goals. Explore your spirituality and connect yourself to your existence. Finally, do what you have always been meant to do. Embrace your greatness.

You're beyond enough. You're completely worthy of acceptance and inner peace. We will discuss these concepts in depth throughout these chapters and you'll have a stronger understanding of how to fully love yourself and live your best life.

> "Doubt kills more dreams than failure ever will."
>
> - SUZY KASSEM

CHAPTER ONE

Clear Out All Areas Of Doubt

What are your favorite things about your life? Think for a moment about what you're grateful for. It's possible to feel that gratitude in each moment of the day. Imagine how it might feel to dive into life and pursue your true potential!

What do your days look like? What kind of people are in your life? What is your profession? What hobbies do you make time for?

You have the opportunity at any moment to take hold of your life in order to create the structure that works for you. This book is going to give you the tools that can help you begin to make changes in your life. You can develop your life however you want.

By practicing new skills and applying new concepts, you will find yourself coming out of your shell in new ways. You will love yourself in a way that makes you feel confident, worthy, and grateful. Learning about and applying self-compassion can revolutionize your lifestyle and help you live your very best life.

SHEDDING YOUR DOUBT

Carrying around negativity and doubt adds a ton of weight to your shoulders. You're allowed to let go and move on from any doubt you have in your life. It's okay to be unsure and confused. That's a natural part of life.

Now you have the opportunity to begin awareness of where you have doubts. You can practice self-awareness by doing daily introspection. How do you feel when you think about work? How do you feel when you think about the relationships in your life? How do you feel about how you spend your time?

Considering these questions and paying attention to how you feel can assist in the objective observation of your daily life and inner dialogue. Your life has many components, and doubt can fester in all of them. The time has come to acknowledge those doubts and take action to be free of them.

SELF-DOUBT

Self-doubt is the first thing you want to let go of. If you're constantly doubting what you say or do, the time has come to make a change. If you lack confidence in any environment, it's time to transform your thinking.

Your spirit and energy can be totally drained by self-doubt. Sometimes it's difficult to realize that you're doubting yourself, especially if self-doubt has become such a natural part of your inner dialogue that you don't notice it.

Let's start by identifying how you doubt yourself and how that doubt manifests in your life.

Questions to consider:

- How often do you sacrifice your needs for what others

want?
- Do you frequently apologize for things you don't need to apologize for?
- Have you ever been called or referred to yourself as a people pleaser?
- Do you stop yourself from speaking up for yourself?

Considering these questions can help reveal any self-doubt you hold that you might not notice.

When you sacrifice your needs for others, you're putting yourself second and neglecting your own importance. When you apologize for what you don't need to, you're shaming yourself and discrediting yourself unnecessarily. You don't need to apologize for passing someone in the hallway or for asking a question.

If you find that you want everyone to like you, you might be a people pleaser. Do you go out of your way to win people over? Do you say things that contradict your values in order to gain the approval of others? This is a good demonstration of self-doubt.

You're allowed to stand tall. You're allowed to speak your truth and be heard. The first step is to raise your self-awareness. Start noticing how much you value yourself compared to those around you. How does your self-doubt manifest in your behavior?

CRITICAL SELF-TALK

Self-doubt can be caused by the words you say to yourself on a daily basis. The way you see yourself and the world around you is affected by your self-talk.

When you're walking into a nerve-racking situation, are you calming yourself in a self-compassionate way? Or are you speaking poorly to yourself about who you are and how the future will turn out?

Telling yourself that you're not enough will weigh heavily on you. Critical self-talk decreases motivation and increases unproductivity in all areas of your life.

If you don't begin to change your thinking, it will be difficult to see the many possibilities in your life. If you continue to berate yourself for the way you walk, talk, or breathe, you will only dig yourself further into a hole of negativity.

So, begin by observing your behavior and actions throughout the day. Hear your self-talk and determine whether it's positive and self-compassionate.

Negative self-talk goes hand-in-hand with self-doubt because they fuel each other. When you doubt yourself, you're not seeing yourself as worthy. When you don't believe you're worthy, you will feel self-doubt.

DOUBTING RELATIONSHIPS

Think about your community as a whole. Take an aerial view of it and see all of the connections in your life. Think about your customer service at your local shopping center or coffee shop, your colleagues at work, your best friends, and any significant other you either have or will have in your life. Do you need more authentic connections in your life?

Begin pursuing the relationships you crave that will add meaning and purpose to your life.

Look at the connections you have with those around you. Do you feel motivated by the people close to you? Do you feel motivated by the people you work with? What's most important is the quality of your relationships.

Are there relationships in your life that you doubt? Begin by getting curious about what is underneath your doubt. How do you feel? Fearful? Resentful? Misunderstood? There are certain things you can do to improve the quality of the relationships in your life. It's okay to crave connection. Humans are wired for that.

It's okay to doubt any relationships. You can either choose to let those relationships go with compassion, or you can decide to commit a conscious effort to make those relationships more beneficial to you.

How to Improve Personal Relationships:

- **Remain patient and compassionate.** If you have a tendency to react strongly, instead, push the pause button to get back to a place of calm and compassion. Express your caring feelings by having an open mind and listening ears.
- **Actively listen.** When you're having a conversation with someone close to you, be sure to give them the floor. Instead

of thinking about what you want to say next, pay attention to what the person in front of you is saying. Show them that you're listening by having open body language and validating their truth.

- **Structure regular times during which you give attention to your relationships.** You can go out and do an activity, make a phone call, or go get a quick coffee. The important thing is to stay in touch and reach out consistently.
- **Learn from the people closest to you.** Just as those in your community can learn from you, you can learn from those in your community. Whether you're discussing your life story or learning about their line of work, there is always something to gain from those around you.
- **Spend time around those who are positive and motivate you.** If you're feeling exhausted by the relationships in your life, see what you can do to liven them up. You can also put yourself out there and meet others who will bring you to new heights.

When you're riddled with doubt, you're probably in a pretty foggy state of mind. It isn't easy to see clearly when your reality is tinted with insecurity and lack of confidence. This is how many people live their whole lives. You don't have to live this way!

Your feelings of doubt likely come from your previous years of errors, shame, and confusion. It's possible to reverse this thinking in a way that will free you from insecurity and help you focus on what is really in front of you in the moment.

Start by working on your thoughts. Do you find yourself overthinking when you're in social situations or after you send a text message to a love interest? It can be difficult to slow down thoughts when they feel like they're going a million miles per minute.

The next chapter will give you some solutions for what to do when you cannot stop overthinking things.

"Don't get too deep, it leads to over thinking, and over thinking leads to problems that don't even exist in the first place."

- JAYSON ENGAY

CHAPTER TWO

Avoid Overthinking

Do you ever try to write your thoughts, but they're coming too quickly for you to write them down? Do you have that feeling of overwhelming thoughts frequently? How much time do you spend ruminating on the past?

Imagine a day where you take each moment as it comes and don't think about past moments. Imagine going to sleep at night without replaying all the wrong things you said that day. This freedom is totally possible by practicing a few new things and applying some principles to your daily life.

We all have a little nagging voice in the back of our head that can tend to narrate negative things regularly. That little nagging voice might convince you that you can tell exactly what others are thinking of you. When you believe these things, you're only creating more destruction in your own life.

Instead of replaying each conversation you've ever had, focus your attention on the present moment. When we remember the past, we typically see more negative than positive.

LETTING GO OF THE PAST

What conversations or behaviors do you think about when you're replaying negativity in your head? Are there people you actively avoid because you're afraid of what they think of you?

Now is the moment where you can let yourself let go of all of those things and move forward. You no longer need to ruminate over the past. Are there memories that make you sad, angry, or fearful for the future? You can let these things go by releasing your regrets and turning them into a tool for positive growth.

HOW TO LET GO OF REGRET

Follow these strategies:

1. **Get curious about what, exactly, you regret.** Do you regret old relationships, decisions, behaviors, or words? The regrets that cause you the most distress are important to dissolve.

2. **Write about your biggest regrets.** Get them apart from you so that you can look at them. Get specific about what you regret. Consider your lifestyle, behavior toward others, or decisions. Do this nonjudgmentally.

3. **Look at these regrets and think about what lessons you can learn from them.** Maybe you can apply one of these situations to your values. You don't need to use regrets to try to be perfect. Instead, you can look at them as opportunities to learn something new about yourself in a positive way.

4. **Practice self-forgiveness.** Give yourself permission to forgive yourself and grow forward. Imagine the shackles of your past dissolving. You will naturally struggle from time to time, and that's okay.

5. **Decide how to move forward.** Though you cannot control every aspect of life, you can control the decisions you make based on your present moment. You don't need to hide away in shame or continue to doubt yourself. Instead, rise up and embrace each moment with a stronger sense of compassion for yourself.

Let your compassion for others grow. Regret helps us feel compassion for others because we can put ourselves in their shoes when sharing difficulties, even if we are on different paths. So, when you're stuck in feelings of regret, you can instantly relate to all who have felt what you feel.

You grow through both your struggles and successes. You can use these moments of regret to re-energize your efforts to live your fullest life and love yourself completely.

THAT LITTLE NAGGING VOICE

Have you noticed any constant chatter in your head that can put a negative tint on your day? What do you do during times of frustration with yourself? You have the power to confront this voice in the back of your head that tells you that you're not enough. You can insist on the opposite, and you're right.

Start by simply hearing what you say to yourself each day, through each interaction and situation.

Think about how your motivation relates to the way you're

speaking to yourself each day. When you're in a good mood, how do you talk to yourself? When you're in a bad mood and having a terrible day, observe how the way you speak to yourself changes or stays the same.

You can adjust the way you talk to yourself by replacing the negative thoughts you think with positive thoughts. It can be as simple as that. Simply come up with a thought that will oppose your critical self-talk.

For example, if you say, "I'm just going to keep disappointing people," you can replace that thought with, "I am growing each day."

This type of resetting the way you treat yourself will have a hugely positive long-term effect. You will notice your thoughts becoming more positive. Pay attention to how your mood changes as a result.

SOCIAL ANXIETY

Do you overthink every social interaction you have? How do you feel when you're approaching a large group of people? Some people thrive more when they are surrounded by people. Others need some quiet time to recharge. Think about how you feel when you're in large groups.

It's common for our thoughts to speed up in social situations because we're paying attention to so many different things. The larger the crowd, the more there is to pay attention to. This can be overwhelming.

Luckily, there are simple things you can do to help ease any social anxiety you feel, regardless of the situation.

These strategies will help minimize social fear:

1. **Get curious about your fear.** Is there something specific that you're afraid will happen? Consider the feelings you feel when you think about an upcoming social situation. What emotions arise when you're walking through a crowd or having a one-on-one coffee with someone?

2. **Walk yourself through that fear by getting rational.** You cannot predict the future. Bring yourself to the present moment and acknowledge that you can choose to assume this will be a good experience, or you can choose to assume it will be a negative experience.

3. **Be compassionate with yourself.** All moments are good times to unconditionally love yourself.

4. **Ask a friend to go with you to social situations that make you nervous.** You and your friend will have a stronger bond, you will do something fun together, and you will have a chance to embrace socializing with a new energy.

When you can move past this fear, you can expand your horizons even further. Continue to grow your self-compassion by moving through fear and getting curious about it, rather than shying away from anything that might be out of your comfort zone.

When you truly believe that you're worthy, you will find many of your common irrational fears drift away. As these fears dissipate, you will find yourself feeling more open and willing to have new experiences and adventures.

GETTING OVER OVERTHINKING

Once you move past your negative thinking, you can begin to explore new arenas of your life. In order to best make these changes, free yourself from your negative self-talk and regret. Acknowledge the people around you and begin to open yourself up to new experiences.

When you have let go of self-doubt and begun to build your relationship with yourself, you will find that you don't ruminate negatively on your day, your past, or your future.

Next, your readiness to embrace the world around will give you new opportunities to thrive.

"I know there is strength in the differences between us. I know there is comfort, where we overlap."

- ANI DIFRANCO

CHAPTER THREE

Explore Your Community

Shedding self-doubt and letting go of overthinking will leave you with more motivation and confidence. When you truly appreciate yourself, fear will not hold you back in the ways that it can in times of self-loathing.

With this freedom, you can pursue activities and people that will fit into the life you want to live.

JUMP IN

Increase your understanding of the world around you by exploring more of it. This does not have to be taxing or time-consuming. You can start exactly where you are.

Start by observing what is around you throughout your day.

Put your phone down while you're in public places, such as the grocery store or the bookstore. You can use these moments to participate in the world around you. Look at your surroundings, at the people around you, and observe yourself in this arena. Keep your head up and try to stay open to those around you.

By showing any willingness to engage in your community, you're opening yourself up to new opportunities for connection. People are typically not as scary as we make them up to be in our heads. By attending local events and activities, you will have the opportunity to have a good time with new people while doing something you enjoy.

Consider these activities for getting involved with the world around you:

1. **Be a tourist in your own town.** Spend a weekend seeing the local attractions your town has to offer. Whether it's large or small, pick an adventure and go with it. You can take a walking tour, go to a museum, or participate in a larger group activity.
2. **Participate in a team sport.** If you love getting active by playing your favorite sport, find a local recreational team that you can join. This will help you get to know people while doing something that you already enjoy.
3. **Try something new.** If you've never done a team sport, try one! If you've never been to a nice restaurant by yourself, try it! You can practice self-compassion while being kind and open to those around you.
4. **Acknowledge the people you see frequently.** If you have the same barista three days per week, or you see the same person at the gas station every time, acknowledge them. Though you hardly play a role in each other's lives, you can always uplift each other's days by having a pleasant interaction.
5. **Learn a new language.** Take a class or join a group that can help you pick up a new language. Choose a language that's frequently spoken around you so that you can connect with more people. You can also choose a language of a country that you plan to visit.

6. **Join a club.** Look online to find groups meeting in your area. You can find groups for everything. Whether you like sewing, reading, painting, or protesting, you can find a group doing just that. This will help you connect with others that you have something in common.

By embracing what's around you, you can use your environment to help you thrive. Living your best life means putting yourself out there in new ways. Do the things you love and learn the things you've always wanted to learn. Shed self-doubt so that you can have frequent moments of fearless connection with others and your world.

BE AUTHENTIC

It is not always easy to be authentic. Being authentic requires that you reveal your true thoughts, dreams, and ideas. Gone are the days of people-pleasing. You can speak up for yourself, pursue the things you want, and talk with new people all while being totally authentic and kind.

Be nice to yourself and kind to others. Being your authentic self means that you're showing the world who you really are by being conscious of your actions and taking chances to demonstrate your values and loves.

Follow these tips for embracing authenticity:
1. **Continue to love yourself.** Increase your self-compassion practice by improving the way you speak to yourself

throughout the day. When you're able to accept yourself in your head, that will show on the outside. You will feel confident and worthy. Your thoughts matter.

2. **Make intentional time to get to know your community.** Whether it's once per week or once every few months, get out and get involved. As you continue to follow through on this commitment, it will get easier, and it will definitely be more fun than fear!

3. **Practice gratitude.** Gratitude is an excellent key to authenticity because it helps you get to a place where you feel grateful for your life and everything in it, good or bad. When you're having these feelings of gratitude, you're more likely to feel at peace with yourself.

4. **Do what brings you fulfillment.** Instead of doing or saying what everyone wants you to, take a pause and think about what is most fulfilling for you. That is what authenticity is about. It is just about you being you, exactly as you are. Love yourself for that.

5. **Allow yourself to be inspired.** Take a deep breath of fresh air, stretch your arms above your head, and listen to the sounds you love. When you're feeling inspired, your confidence goes up and you're more comfortable with yourself.

6. **Increase interactions with those around you.** By putting yourself in small, positive social situations, you can have even

more practice with being truly you. Practice on the small stuff, like ordering the food you want to eat for dinner or picking out the movie for your group of friends.

You can build authenticity over time. At first, it can be a tricky concept to work with because sometimes it can be difficult to catch ourselves being inauthentic. If you notice that you're people-pleasing or avoiding your truth, compassionately remind yourself that you have permission to be exactly who you are (and exactly who you are is enough).

Start by noticing the times when you're inauthentic and thinking about what you could do or say differently in future instances. For example, if you choose music that you don't like because you know your friend would like it, you can decide that next time you will play the music you want to listen to.

Doing this on small things will build confidence to speak up when it really counts.

LET GO OF EXPECTATIONS

When you go out to a large concert or even a small dinner, do you find that you begin to play everything that you think might happen while you're out? Do you imagine negative conversations, rejection, or a negative memory being formed?

When you're excited about something, do you find yourself imagining how perfect it will be? Do you ever find yourself disappointed when things don't live up to your expectations? This is totally normal.

As humans, we crave certainty. It sometimes seems easier to assume that the worst will happen than to accept that we have no idea what will happen. There is something a bit insecure about letting go of expectations. It can feel like a lack of structure or security.

LET GO OF PERFECTION

First, let's talk about the disappointment that comes when things don't meet our expectations. Imagine you're attending a party and expect to have so much fun, taking photos, laughing, and having the best night of your life. Your expectations set up your excitement for the entire night.

If you have expectations that things will be perfect, you will crash to disappointment as soon as things stop being perfect, even if they are still going well. Sometimes expectations are crushed even after a night that has gone wonderfully. Because it was not the perfect, exciting night you imagined, you feel a loss.

When you find your mind drifting toward expectations of perfection, take these moments as a sign that it's time to pause and release these expectations. Instead, you can say, "I am excited for what this evening holds," with a sense of curiosity instead of pressure.

If you find yourself disappointed when things did not go according to plan, reflect on the event and find what did go well. Maybe things that you had not even considered in your planning went well. Maybe it was just one thing that made the whole night seem terrible.

LET GO OF THE WORST-CASE SCENARIO

It's easy to assume that the worst is going to happen.

For example, when you need to give an important speech, you might find yourself assuming that you're going to be a total failure. You may be putting unnecessary pressure on yourself to be outstanding, and you may find yourself assuming that you cannot live up to the greatness that you want to live up to.

If you're going on a first date, you might assume that your date will be horrible and that they will not like you.

How could you possibly know? By walking into situations with these negative attitudes, you're more likely to feel stress and fear while you're in that moment.

If you feel like the worst is going to happen, pause for a moment to remind yourself that you cannot tell the future. Remind yourself that you get to control yourself and your behaviors, no matter the situation. So, you can choose to walk into a new situation with a patient curiosity and an open mind.

Negative mindsets often take years to develop. It may be a habit that you picked up in an attempt to protect yourself from previous fears. You can find the beliefs that are not productive for you and choose to release them.

So, if you're assuming that people don't like you or that things are not going to go your way, you can dive into that and learn more.

FOCUS ON THE MOMENT

Letting go of expectations will enable you to live your best life because it's another layer of weight that you're removing from the things that keep you from being truly you.

Instead of having any expectations at all, positive or negative, learn to embrace the present moment for exactly what it is. You don't have to obsess over the past or try to predict the future. You don't have to try to read people's minds or try to predict their behavior.

Instead, take a pause and bring yourself to the present moment. This present moment acknowledgment comes as a result of mindfulness and can be applied to every area of your life, every day.

> "Be mindful. Be grateful. Be positive. Be true. Be kind."
>
> - ROY T. BENNETT

CHAPTER FOUR

Practice Mindfulness

Mindfulness is simply awareness of the present moment.

It's common to think frequently about the past and the future. You replay your day, remember childhood disappointment, and grapple with loss. You try to predict the future, assume the worst, expect perfection, or get disappointed before the next thing has even happened.

How often do you stop thinking about the past or the future and instead consciously focus your attention on the here and now?

Mindfulness means you're giving your full mind to the present moment. There are many ways to practice mindfulness, and we will go over many of them here.

Mindfulness will have a powerful effect on your mind and your life. You will find that you have stronger emotion regulation, feel more at peace throughout the day, and enjoy yourself more than ever before.

Your self-compassion practice will be drastically improved when you begin to put mindfulness in your routine. Practicing mindfulness is helpful with self-compassion because it helps center you in reality and feel calm and accepting of everything around you, including yourself.

Living your fullest life means taking each moment as it comes. You can appreciate every moment and look for each lesson.

MINDFULNESS

Mindfulness nonjudgmentally invites you into the present moment. When you can sit in the present moment and have compassion and open-mindedness, you will be able to connect to yourself on a truly self-compassionate level.

When you're truly mindful, you will find a new peace of mind that brings about calm throughout your life and your heart.

Mindfulness is simply turning your attention toward the present moment. You can do this by implementing some practices to help you bring your mind to a present state.

It's a good idea to make time each day to practice mindfulness. You can begin by working on doing your typical routines in a more mindful way.

For example, you can mindfully brush your teeth by taking your time instead of rushing through.

Begin by getting your toothbrush wet and putting toothpaste on it. Notice your tube of toothpaste and the color of your toothbrush. You can do all of this without judging any of it as "good" or "bad." Begin brushing your teeth. Pay attention to the bristles on the brush. Notice the taste of the toothpaste and feel your teeth getting cleaner.

Pay attention to any tension you're holding. Relax your shoulders and jaw. Loosen your grip on your toothbrush a little bit.

If you begin your day like this each morning, you'll begin to notice a change. This is an excellent way to start your day and a great way to implement mindfulness.

You can find many ways to practice mindfulness. There are many avenues toward compassion and awareness of the present moment. Try many activities to find ways that work for you to practice mindfulness.

Consider these simple mindfulness activities:
1. **Body Scan.** You can release tension and come back to the center of the present moment by checking your body for tightness. Do this by sitting comfortably or laying on your back. Begin at your toes and work your way up to your body, relaxing each of your muscles as you go.
2. **Pay attention to your five senses.** Name things you hear, see, feel, taste, or smell. By doing this, you're remaining observant of where you are right now, and you're connecting yourself to this moment.
3. **Practice mindfulness meditation.** You can simply sit and pay attention to your breathing. You don't have to breathe in a particular way. Simply notice your breath.
    - Avoid judging intruding thoughts. Acknowledge them and then return your attention to your breathing.
4. **Mindfully eat your favorite food.** Sit with your plate in front of you. Look at all of the food and smell the delicious smells. When you take a bite, pay close attention to the taste and texture of each food.

5. **Color in a coloring book.** Coloring is an excellent mindfulness skill. It's fun and it's a great way to get your energy out without acting on it in a negative way. Pay attention to the colors and all of the shapes you're coloring. You can set a timer for 15 minutes of coloring and see how relaxed you feel at the end.

With all mindfulness activities, your thoughts will likely drift. If they do, simply come back to the moment. You never need to judge yourself for getting lost in thought again.

When you're truly mindful, you have no judgments on anything. You're able to simply sit in the moment and tolerate what you're going through. Mindfulness brings more enjoyment to each moment.

When you can truly appreciate this, you will find compassion blossoming. Having compassion in the present moment connects mindfulness to self-compassion. Self-compassion and mindfulness work together to create a full love for self and life.

MINDFULNESS AND SELF-COMPASSION

When you're able to truly be in the moment, you will have easy access to a deep well of self-compassion and compassion for everyone. When you're sitting in the present moment, pay attention to having compassion for the moment. Take that compassion and turn it inward.

Self-compassion comes when you're able to truly give yourself the love and appreciation you need. When you're practicing self-compassion, you're embracing each part of you in every moment.

When you're mindful in the moment, take your attention to yourself. If judgments or regrets come up, simply respond with deep self-compassion. What would you say to your very best friend?

If you're suffering, how do you speak to yourself? If you made a mistake or lost an opportunity, how would you speak to yourself? In times when you're being critical of yourself, you can use mindfulness skills to increase your self-compassion and be better able to tolerate the present moment.

One effective way to arrive back at self-compassion is by taking a self-compassion break.

To begin, take a few deep breaths. Relax your shoulders and ease the tension in your jaw. Give yourself a hug and comfort yourself. Give yourself all of the kindness that you would give to your closest friend. Allow yourself to feel loved and grounded in the present moment.

CONSTANTLY COMPASSIONATE

When you've found self-compassion for yourself, you can begin to spread that compassion to all beings. Imagine your compassion growing and growing. By starting small with mindfulness, you will see all of the ways you can implement it in your life. Over time, you can continue to advance your practice and find even more appreciation for the present moment.

As your self-compassion grows, so will your compassion for all beings. Imagine your compassion growing and growing until it encompasses the earth with love. You can feel that peace and calm by having a regular and consistent mindfulness practice.

Giving yourself compassionate attention can transform your life.

"Letting go means to come to the realization that some people are a part of your history, but not a part of your destiny."

- STEVE MARABOLI

CHAPTER FIVE

Let Go Of What Holds You Back

Moving forward means letting go of the past. We can be grateful for what we've learned and gained from the past. However, staying in it and wishing to change it, or remaining resentful for many years, will stunt your personal growth.

There are many things you can move on from. In order to best glide forward and reach new heights of happiness and success, there are people to forgive, fears to move on from, and negative people to let go of. You can even let go of yourself and forgive yourself. Set yourself free from all of these things.

LET GO OF RESENTMENT

Resentment is one of the heaviest things you can carry with you. It limits genuine freedom. People can be unjust and hurtful. You never have to be okay with what anyone has done. When someone has done something to hurt you or someone you love, you're allowed to be angry.

The fact is what happened is what happened. That is the first step to forgiveness. Practice radical acceptance. Begin by acknowledging that the reality is indeed the reality. Acknowledge it mindfully, without judgment.

All you need to say is, "Yes, this happened." This is acceptance. Acceptance does not mean that you're okay with what happened.

Acceptance will enable you to move forward from resentment.

Once you've come to acceptance, you can begin the process of forgiveness. Despite how you may feel, forgiveness does not require the person you're upset with to do anything. Forgiveness is all about you. As with all things, forgiving becomes easier with practice.

First, write down your resentments in a list. Begin with the people who are easiest to forgive, and work from there. When a person comes up who you want to forgive, you can take a deep breath and say, "I forgive you." While you're doing this, release tension in your body and allow yourself to relax and feel the resentment leaving.

You will need to do this process for some people multiple times.

Forgiveness is powerfully beneficial and will make your life more joyful and rewarding.

This is also a great opportunity to learn more about yourself. Use your feelings of resentment and your process of forgiveness to get to know yourself better. How can this inform your values? Where do you want to go from here?

LET GO OF FEAR

Most fears are imaginary. They are stories we tell ourselves about who we are and what is going to happen.

When you feel fearful of the future, you keep yourself from achieving your fullest truth. You have learned fear. At some point, fear has served you. Of course, there are rational fears. The fears to let go of are the ones you think of when you think of what fears are holding you back from being truly you.

When you imagine your fullest self, what fears have you shed? What fears are long forgotten? It's helpful to visualize yourself feeling this freedom. These feelings will motivate you to make your fullest life a reality.

When you find yourself feeling fearful, observe and name that fear. Use your rational mind to understand what fears are coming from your ego.

Observe the moments when you feel fearful. Then, watch what you do in response to that fear. Begin working on remaining open during these times of fear. Instead of closing off and going back into your shell, see what it's like to remain open even in the face of fear.

You have much courage within you. When you feel fear creep in, name it, sit with it, and release it. Being mindful in these moments is essential. Bring yourself to the present moment. Breathe in your courage, exhale your fear. Imagine the fear leaving your body and leaving you only with greater courage.

LET GO OF NEGATIVE PEOPLE

Are the relationships in your life serving you well? It's easy to get lost in a destructive relationship. Sometimes it's easier to stay friends with someone than it would be to stop being friends with them.

Remember, there are many people around you who relate to and appreciate you. The only way to find them is by loving yourself fully and putting yourself into the world around you.

The way you let people treat you says a lot about how you treat yourself. If you begin being kinder to yourself, you may find that you're better able to ask for what you need from those around you.

When you can ask for what you need from others, you're showing yourself respect and love. When you demand respect from others by demonstrating it to yourself, you will find your relationships beginning to improve.

You will know that a relationship is no longer serving you when you leave interactions with that person feeling worse than you did when you arrived. If this happens regularly, or you see a pattern of inconsistent behavior, or even if it's simply a difference in values, you might want to consider letting go of that relationship.

It can be intimidating to cut ties with a friend. However, it's a necessary part of growth. Sometimes you only need to be in someone's life for a short time so that you can both learn what you need to. You don't need to be friends with all of your friends forever.

One way to create structure around the kind of people you allow in your life is by setting boundaries. If you have a toxic friendship in your life, you can put boundaries in place to keep your needs clear.

For example, if you have a friend who is frequently intoxicated when you're together, and that upsets you, you can set a boundary that you will not spend time with that friend when they are intoxicated.

This boundary is clear and not up for interpretation.

Setting boundaries like these can help keep your toxic relationships at bay, and new positive relationships will come forward.

HOW TO SET BOUNDARIES

Try these techniques:

1. **Get quiet and think about your needs.** You can write on a piece of paper about what you need in your life and what people are no longer helping you attain your greatest good. Let yourself write without judgment and see what feelings or needs come to the surface.

2. **Establish your limits.** Know where the line is for how much you're willing to tolerate.

3. **Know what you need.** In times of stress or frustration with a person, what are things that you need in those moments, based on how you feel? Do you need to leave? Do you need to end the interaction?

4. **Communicate your boundaries clearly.** Boundaries are a great guidepost because they are sturdy and you can simply repeat that boundary in response to any reaction you get back.

5. **Be consistent in following through on your boundaries.** Pay attention to how you feel when you do or don't follow through. If it's difficult for you to take a stand, keep practicing and see

what happens.

6. **Give yourself the okay to let go of these people that are causing harm or limiting you.**

ALLOW YOURSELF TO LET GO

Now, give yourself permission to do all the healing and let go that you need to. In order to most powerfully grow forward, you must commit to trusting the process fully. You can now let go of your past. You can let go of your regret, anger, fear. You can let go of the people that hold you back or don't believe in who your best self is.

When you're letting go of people, you can take that time to participate in your community in ways that will help you get closer to people who are better suited for this season in your life.

"When you truly love or want what you are pursuing, holding on can never be harder than giving up."

-MOKOKOMA MOKHONOANA

CHAPTER SIX

Hold On To What Moves You Forward

When you let go of one thing, you're free to hold onto another. As you let go of the things that hold you back, you're now able to grab hold of the things that will propel you forward.

There are many things you can use to help move you forward. Start with the things that inspire you most and work from there.

In this chapter, we'll cover some great things you can begin to hold that will help you continue to grow. What is meaningful in your life and how can you pursue it? How can you use spirituality to ground you and move you forward? How can you best embrace positive experiences and give yourself what you need in your daily routines?

CLARIFY YOUR VALUES

Take a moment to think about the most important things to you. Think of your family, friends, work, and yourself. What words come up when you think about these things? What words come up when you think about what kind of person you want to be? These things are what you value.

You can narrow down your values to just a few core values that can help guide you in the right direction toward a fulfilling life. You can determine your values however you want to. What character traits would you most like to act on? Honesty? Humor? Integrity? Leadership? Family?

Think large, and then get smaller. Come up with a large list of values and then narrow it down. Think of about 4 - 5 values that you want to live up to on a daily basis.

Once you have those values selected, begin thinking about what it might look like if you put these values into action. For example, what would you do more of if you followed your value of humor? What would you do less of if you lived up to your value of family?

Imagine yourself acting out these values and keep them in mind as you go about your days.

Use these values when you're trying to make a decision about what the next right thing is. Use them to determine what sort of people you want to invite into your life. You can even use your values to give you confidence and meaning.

When you have a solid set of values, so many things will fall into place. Values make things straightforward and clear.

You will typically be able to tell if you're not living up to your values. Just as in mindfulness, when you find yourself straying from your values, nonjudgmentally come back to them.

Having your values solidified will help guide you through the rest of your life. You can start to set goals that will help you grow at exponential rates.

GOAL SETTING

Set goals that are realistic for you and that are based on your values. You can use your values to help you determine where you want to end up. When you bring your dreams into the mix, goals, start to appear.

Set long-term goals first. Think of your wildest dreams and then work from there to come up with some short-term goals that will help you in your day-to-day life.

Goals will help guide you to your true potential. You'll be better able to see the big picture when you know what you're really working for. When you don't have a big idea in mind, it can be easy to lose perspective.

By keeping your long-term dreams in mind, you'll be able to take a step back and see your purpose any time that you're feeling lost. Goals are the breadcrumbs that lead to the dream.

EXPLORE SPIRITUALITY

If you can get to a place of peace and calm with the meaning of your existence, you will feel much more at peace in the rest of your life. No matter what your spirituality entails, you can choose how you want to tether yourself to your existence.

What brings you peace in the storm? What can you learn from each moment of your life? Imagine the things that bring you the most comfort. When do you feel the most connected to the world around you?

These methods will help you explore your spirituality:

1. **Go somewhere peaceful and sit quietly or write.** Think about a time or two when you've felt the most connected to the world around you. Think about a time when you've felt truly connected to your feelings of meaning in your life.
2. **Look at the core of those moments.** What were you feeling? What were you doing? What were you trusting?
3. **Now, go do more of those things.** If you enjoy sitting outside, go sit outside. Doing things that help you connect to nature is an excellent way to get to a spiritual place.
4. **Volunteer.** When you help others, you will feel a sense of calm that is rarely found elsewhere. This type of authentic human connection can improve your relationship with your ideas of spirituality.
5. **Practice mindfulness.** Practicing mindfulness daily is a great way to get more in touch with your spirituality. Sitting in that stillness can bring about transcendental experiences that can help you grow in new ways.
6. **Talk with others about spirituality.** If there are people in your life whom you admire, you can discuss their spirituality with them. Ask them how their spirituality informs the rest of their life.

You can use your feeling of spiritual purpose to ignite and bring calming inspiration to all areas of your life.

Having a larger idea of why you're here will help center you in the present moment and give you a stronger sense of security when you're full of existential angst. Holding onto spiritual habits that work for you will bring a new sense of strength to your life and your heart.

EMBRACE YOUR GREATNESS

Praise yourself each day and embrace the greatness that you truly are. When you truly begin to realize that you're completely worthy of love, you will also realize that you're unstoppable.

Feel your sense of greatness well up within you. During moments of mindfulness practice, feel your back straighten and your shoulders relax. Feel the inspiration flowing in your veins and enjoy the person you are.

Start by treating yourself when you need to. What are your favorite things to do? Start making time each day or each week to do the things that you love most. You deserve to have fun, and you can give yourself that fun by taking charge and believing in your worthiness.

Make kindness a regular part of your daily self-talk. You can do many things to remain in a place of compassion with yourself. For example, write yourself short and encouraging notes in the morning. You can use these to motivate you through the rest of the day. Who says you cannot tell yourself that you're proud of yourself?

Give yourself praise each day. You're allowed to praise yourself for getting out of bed, putting on shoes, or getting a promotion. Be proud of yourself for everything. You've worked hard to get where you are. By giving yourself praise, you're acknowledging your strengths and giving validation to yourself.

"For us to feel good emotionally, we have to look after ourselves."

- SAM OWEN

SUMMARY

Self-compassion is a lifelong project and a daily practice. By loving yourself fully, the real you will come to the surface and you'll have a stronger understanding of the beauty within your life. By seeing this beauty, you'll be better able to live your most fulfilling life.

Shed the doubt that you hold onto. What self-doubt do you carry around with you? How does it affect your behavior? When you're able to see the areas in which you doubt yourself, you can begin changing self-sabotaging behavior that keeps you from your best self.

If there are relationships that are struggling in your life, you can either let them go or try to improve them. Doing nothing will not make anything better. You can improve your relationships with friends, community members, colleagues, and family by being patient and compassionate.

Showing compassion for others will help you practice it for yourself, just as being compassionate to yourself makes it easier to show compassion to others.

If you consider yourself an overthinker, you can bring your mind to a state of peace by shedding the various ways in which you overthink.

Let go of the past. Let go of the things you've done that you feel guilty for.

Let go of regret. You can let go of regret by giving yourself permission to move forward. Write about the things you regret in order to take a step back and learn from them. There is always a lesson to learn if you're willing to look for it.

Use moments of regret as an opportunity for connection to all those who have experienced what you're feeling.

Release that little nagging voice.

You're your biggest bully. You no longer need to say harsh things to yourself in times of confusion or doubt. Perhaps you've noticed a constant narrator that is sometimes (or frequently) negative and destructive. There's no need for you to listen to this voice, as it only keeps you from pursuing your greatest self.

Instead of listening to the negative things you say to yourself, replace those things with positive phrases and thoughts. Instead of believing that you're a failure, see yourself as a learner.

Social anxiety and fears are common and necessary to move through if you want to adventure through life with openness. However, letting go of these fears can be difficult. You can begin by asking a friend to help you through social situations that make you nervous.

Jump into the adventure of the community around you. Peruse your community with the eyes of an explorer. Dive in and see what is in store. Take a quiet moment to truly participate in the world around you.

You can engage with your community by talking with others and being kind to them. Building community starts small. Starting small helps you build confidence in approaching new people if that is something that makes you nervous.

You can get involved with the world around you by being a tourist in your own town, trying something new with a group of people, or having a conversation with the barista at your coffee shop.

When you're diving into your community, do so with authenticity. The more you love yourself, the more comfortable you will be with being authentic. Increase the interactions with the people around you so that you can continue to practice being your true self and connecting with people from that level.

Let go of expectations. These expectations don't serve you. Instead, bring your attention to the present moment, where all is well and you're full of gratitude.

Mindfulness is an essential part of uncovering your true self-compassion.

You can practice mindfulness by paying close attention to what you're doing in the present moment. Choose an activity that works for you and make it a regular part of your daily routines. Use mindfulness to grow your self-compassion practice by loving yourself in each moment.

Let go of the things that keep you from growing.

By letting go of the things that no longer serve you, you're freeing yourself to experience life on entirely different levels. Let go of resentment, fear, and negative people. When you let go of resentment, you're releasing a weight off your shoulders that you may not have noticed before because it has been there for so long.

When you let go of fear, you're better able to fully embrace the future with curiosity. You will be better able to approach the present moment with a built-in sense of gratitude. When you feel fear creep in, remain mindful and express compassion for that fear while you release it.

Let go of negative people by setting clear boundaries with them. Get your needs clear and establish your limits. Give yourself what you need by recognizing your specific needs in stressful situations where you may need to have strict boundaries. Communicate your boundaries clearly and continue to follow through on them.

Take hold of the things that propel you in a healthy direction.

By embracing your true self, you can let go of the patterns that are not helpful for you. When you let go of those things, you can hold onto more positive things.

Get clear with your values so that you can use them as a compass on your journey in a fulfilling life. Look to your values to help point you in the right direction when you're not sure where to go. Your values determine the kind of person you want to be and how you want your behavior to reflect that.

Set realistic goals that are based on your wildest dreams.

Determine what small thing you can do each day to work toward those dreams. Set goals each day, week, or month in order to keep yourself moving forward.

Acknowledge your greatness.

When you're able to look in the mirror and feel truly proud of who you see, you will know this practice is working. You can appreciate yourself, and you should.

You're allowed to be proud of yourself and grateful for what a great person you are. Take this deep love for yourself and find security in it. As you're living at your fullest potential, you're able to move forward and grow to new levels of knowledge.

When you love yourself, you can live fully.

AFFIRMATION REFLECTIONS
Now is my time to create the life of my dreams.

I am choosing to dust off my dreams and make them happen now! I am ready to become the creator that I came here to be!

I am grateful that I have taken the time to eliminate all fears from my life. I am happy that I have taken the time to eliminate doubt from my life. I am in great appreciation for all the training and education I have taken to get to this point in my life.

Now, I am done procrastinating my joy!

I feel my strength well up inside of me. I feel my courage fill my chest. I am expanding into who I have come here to be!

I feel the wind under my wings. I feel that I can fly! I am feeling the support of the energy of life itself!

I breathe in new confidence. I breathe out anything that fails to serve me. Now is my time! I stand tall in what I am here to do at this time.

I feel a new surge of energy supporting my dreams. I feel I have turned a corner in my life. I feel I have opened a door to a new reality.

All life is working in my favor! I feel that all the planets have aligned, and it is GO TIME!

I release any misgivings of being unworthy of what is my birthright. I let go of any thoughts that inhibit my good. I eliminate old beliefs from my DNA.

Today, I am born again to create the life of my dreams.

Self-Reflection Questions:

1. What do I need to eliminate in order to create the life of my dreams now?
2. Who no longer fits in my new reality that I need to let go of?
3. What stops me from my complete and total good?

_____
_____
_____
_____
_____
_____
_____
_____
_____
_____
_____
_____
_____
_____
_____
_____
_____
_____
_____
_____

Each day, I savor the moments of my life.

Every moment of my day offers me the opportunity for something wonderful. How I choose to look at these moments makes a difference in how I feel. I choose to look at my life as meaningful, peaceful, and joyful.

Whether I am alone or surrounded by others, my life is full of treasured moments. Everyone I meet has the opportunity to join me in the joyous celebration of life! I see the value in all people, no matter who they are.

I bring beauty to my own life and to the lives of others. By savoring my life, I give thanks to the life force that creates and sustains me. Each day I look for things that bring me joy. Every day I find moments I can savor and appreciate.

No matter what is happening in my life, I know I am valuable, and my life has meaning and purpose. Because I see the beauty in my life, I am able to accept what comes to me and appreciate all of it. I am brave and courageous, and I live each moment.

There is so much beauty in life, both in big events and small, quiet happenings. I see beauty everywhere I look and find joy, peace, and love. I attract it from others and radiate it back to the universe to come around again.

Today, I appreciate and make use of every moment I have been given.

Self-Reflection Questions:

1. How can I learn to pay more attention to special moments in my life?
2. What can I do to remember that each moment has value?
3. How should I work toward savoring the experiences that happen to me each day?

_____
_____
_____
_____
_____
_____
_____
_____
_____
_____
_____
_____
_____
_____
_____
_____
_____
_____
_____

Today is my day.

I use my time wisely. I figure out my priorities. I get organized. I act intentionally. I am grateful for each experience and make the most of each day.

I take care of my health and wellbeing. I go to bed early, so I can get 8 hours of sleep each night. I eat healthy and exercise regularly.

I continue learning. I read books and travel. I take courses online or at local universities. I talk with others about their hobbies and careers.

I give generously. Helping others gives me joy and satisfaction. I volunteer in my community. I do yard work and errands for elderly neighbors. I put bird feeders and heated water in my backyard for birds in the winter.

I spend time with my loved ones. I hang out with family and friends. I read to my children and plan weekend outings.

I express my creativity. I work on my hobbies. I draw and paint. I play musical instruments and cook gourmet meals. I work in my garden and redecorate my living room.

I challenge myself. I tackle difficult tasks that help me to grow personally and professionally.

I lighten up. I set aside time to laugh and play. I take relaxing breaks. I see the humor in difficult situations.

Today, I engage in meaningful activities and enjoy each moment I am given. I believe in myself and follow my dreams. I am happy and successful.

Self-Reflection Questions:

1. What is one new thing I want to try today?
2. How can slowing down help me to stop wasting time?
3. What can my children teach me about enjoying life?

Each step I take leads to the life that I want.

I walk with purpose and unshakable confidence. My steps are deliberate and well-thought-out.

My time is a precious commodity. I use it wisely and towards specific purposes. Keeping my eye on my goals encourages me to be mindful of time.

I balance downtime with productivity. I know that each is important to creating balance. It is important for me to know when to apply one over the other.

Taking a break from work gives me the chance to rest and refill my cup of mental wellness. A strong mind is capable of achieving great things. Building mental exercises into each day is a conscious decision.

My greatest resource is my own mind. Giving it time to generate robustness and nimbleness is essential to producing at a high level professionally.

I challenge myself by associating with top minds in business. When I make myself vulnerable to the brilliance of others, I pull myself up another notch. I give credit to the wise people around me because their track record for success is proven.

Building a life of happiness and success requires giving attention to various factors. I humbly accept my experiences and allow them to lift me to higher heights.

Today, moving ahead means humbly accepting the lessons that life presents to me and using them as steppingstones. I commit to recalibrating my steps along the way so that my goals remain in sight.

Self-Reflection Questions:

1. How do I incorporate lessons from roadblocks into my daily life?
2. What could I do differently to preempt and prevent potential challenges?
3. How do I know when to pivot and take a different route towards a goal?

I am bold and courageous.

I am a bold person that loves to take calculated risks. I am willing to take risks that have a worthwhile reward.

Though I am bold, I avoid being foolish. I avoid risks that lack a sufficient payoff. I consider the risks and rewards of all of my decisions.

I am bold enough to try new things. I welcome change into my life and have the boldness to face life head on. I am fearless when the risk is minimal.

I am much bolder than most others. My boldness is one of my strengths, and I use it to my advantage.

My courage comes from within myself. I have faith in my judgement and my abilities. As I accumulate more successes, I am becoming even more courageous. The more my courage grows, the more my life expands.

My confidence is growing, and this fuels my courage. My courage and confidence grow together. More of one leads to more of the other.

I am a highly capable person. I have the right to be confident and brave. I am living my life to the fullest and taking action on a daily basis. I avoid living life on the sidelines. I am a key player in the arena of life.

Today, I am facing my day from a position of boldness and courageousness. I am attacking today with confidence and grit. I am a bold and courageous person.

Self-Reflection Questions:

1. How could I be bolder in my life? What is holding me back?
2. When have I demonstrated courage? What was the result?
3. Who is the most courageous person I know? What can I learn from this person?

_____
_____
_____
_____
_____
_____
_____
_____
_____
_____
_____
_____
_____
_____
_____
_____
_____
_____
_____

I am building my future one day at a time.

I start each day with the intention of building a brighter future. I know that each day is an opportunity to lift my life to a higher level

I make the most of each day by choosing my actions carefully. I recognize that everything I think and do affects my future. Each thought or action can either help bring me the future I want, or it can make that future further away.

I have a clear vision for my future. I have a plan for creating my ideal future one step at a time, and I am following it as closely as I can. My focus is on doing what I can do today to create the future I desire.

I have big plans, and I know that big plans take time.

I am patient, but I am also optimistic. I feel a high degree of certainty that my ideal future is coming to fruition. I am putting in the work and patiently waiting for the results.

I avoid allowing a day to go by without taking active steps to guarantee my future.

Today, I am more focused than ever on my future. I am making the most of this day and accomplishing as much as I can. My decisions are based on my goals. I am building my future one day at a time.

Self-Reflection Questions:

1. What is my vision for the future? Is it appealing, motivating, and precise? How can I make it even better?

2. What steps am I taking each day to make that vision a reality? What else could I be doing?

3. What do I need to remove from my life to improve the odds of being successful?

_____
_____
_____
_____
_____
_____
_____
_____
_____
_____
_____
_____
_____
_____
_____
_____

I am free of the habit of criticizing myself.

I am imperfect, but I do my best each day. Perfection is an unobtainable objective that only leads to constant failure. I congratulate myself each day for giving my best effort in everything I do.

I avoid criticizing myself. The world is challenging enough without making it even more challenging. It is pointless to make my life any more challenging than it needs to be by lowering my self-esteem.

I choose to focus on my positive qualities and simply correct my errors as I move through life. This is an effective way for me to live my life.

I weaken myself when I criticize myself. I feel less capable and less powerful with self-criticism.

I make the decision each day to praise myself and acknowledge my positive qualities. This puts me in a much better mental state that supports happiness and success.

I engage in positive self-talk that strengthens, motivates, and supports me. I deserve to be spoken to in a kind and supportive manner. I want the best for myself, and I speak to myself accordingly.

Today, I am freeing myself from any self-generated criticism. I am focusing on my positive attributes and strengths. I am choosing to see myself in a positive light, and I am accepting my flaws. I am free of the habit of criticizing myself.

Self-Reflection Questions:

1. What do I criticize myself about? What do I think this will accomplish? What negative impact does it have on my life when I criticize myself?
2. What would change in my life if I stopped criticizing myself?
3. What are my positive qualities? What am I good at?

I am free to be myself.

I am comfortable with myself. In fact, I love myself. I am 100% confident with being myself regardless of who is present. I find it easier to be myself than to pretend to be someone else.

I am comfortable in my own skin. I am happy with the person I am and pleased with the person I am becoming. I freely reveal myself to the world.

My strengths are on full display. I am comfortable showing the world my skills, talents, and abilities. I confidently demonstrate my power. I am unafraid to let everyone see just how powerful and capable I am.

I am honest regarding my flaws, mistakes, and weaknesses. I know that everyone is flawed. I avoid pretending that I am perfect.

When I allow others to see my weaknesses, they respect and admire me.

I inspire others to feel free to be themselves. I am helping others when I show that I am comfortable being myself.

Today, I am free of posturing and pretending. I am living a life free of lies. I am free to be myself, and I am helping others to feel that same sense of freedom.

Self-Reflection Questions:

1. What do I keep hidden from the world? Why? What is this costing me socially and personally?

2. How would my life change if I freely shared myself with the world? What is the worst that could happen? What is the best that could happen?

3. How do I feel about other people that are comfortable with who they are? What can I learn from this?

I am full of gratitude.

I have so much to be thankful for. All of my needs and many of my wants are met. People who care about me surround me and I am aware of their loving presence. Because of this, I am full of gratitude.

So many people in this world go without basic needs: food, shelter, or clean water. Many struggle just to get by each day. When I think about these things, I remember how blessed I am. Regardless of what my future may hold, today I have food, shelter, and clean water and those gifts are worthy of my gratitude.

Each day, I take a few moments to remind myself of my many blessings. I think of the people who love me. I take a moment to mentally send love and gratitude to all of them in return.

I remember all of the ways in which life is easy for me. I have gifts and talents to share. Many things come easily to me, even when I feel challenged by my life. Other things come less easily to me, but I know that each one is an opportunity to learn.

I intentionally cultivate thankfulness for life's challenging situations too.

If I ever feel like I have little to be grateful for, and counting my blessings seems not to help, I go out of my way to do a good turn for someone else. By being helpful to others, I remind myself that the world is an abundant place. And when I remember this, I am grateful.

Today, I am thankful for the blessings in my life. I take time to be conscious of each of them. With all of this abundance surrounding me, I am full of gratitude.

Self-Reflection Questions:

1. What can I be thankful for today?
2. How can I be of service to someone today?
3. In what ways does being helpful to others increase my own gratitude?

_____
_____
_____
_____
_____
_____
_____
_____
_____
_____
_____
_____
_____
_____
_____
_____
_____
_____
_____

I am grateful for the abundance that I experience daily.

I am filled with the joy of gratitude for all that I have. I am blessed to have such abundance in my life.

I take time each day to count my many blessings. I am fortunate to enjoy good health, wealth, and happiness. I deserve these things because I act daily to cultivate them. I make my health, finances, and happiness a priority.

My friends and family are another source of abundance. I am the recipient of great love, respect, and admiration. The people in my life are constant reminders of my value to the world. I am innately important and valuable.

Whatever I require, I am provided. All the resources I require to live an exciting and fruitful life are around me. My biggest task is to identify the resources I need and keep my eyes open. Whatever I need is sure to be found quickly and easily. I know what I need, and I know how to get it.

While I enjoy unlimited abundance, I avoid the burden of accumulating excessive possessions. I take what I need and remain free of greedy behavior. Living this way keeps my time and conscience free and unburdened.

Today, I give thanks for all that I have. The bounty of the world is mine to enjoy and use as necessary. I am grateful for the abundance that I experience daily.

Self-Reflection Questions:

1. What do I have in my life that fills me with feelings of gratitude?
2. How can I be more open to receiving abundance into my life?
3. How have I impeded receiving abundance?

I am living my life fully.

I am living my life fully now instead of waiting for some time in the future, like retirement, to enjoy my life.

I avoid waiting for circumstances outside of my control to change. I am living my life full out NOW!

I realize what is within my control. I can be anything I want to be. I can do anything I want to do. I can have anything I want to have. I know all of that is within my control.

I am choosing to live my life. I am taking the bull by the horns and riding that bull!

I am cashing in on all the things on my bucket list NOW!

I am taking the vacations that I always wanted to take. I realize that life is short. I stop putting off my life and live it now!

I am opening myself up to making new friends. I am opening myself up to new opportunities.

I am getting on that surfboard and feeling the exhilaration of living NOW!

I am kicking fear to the curb. I am DONE allowing fear to rule my life.

Today, I am doing things that I have always wanted to do but put off until tomorrow. I see now there is no tomorrow, only today.

Self-Reflection Questions:

1. What fears am I ready to eliminate now?
2. What stops me from going on vacation now?
3. What stops me from claiming my bucket list items now?

I am my own best cheerleader.

I root for myself in all situations. I offer myself praise and appreciate the compliments I give myself. I choose words that motivate me.

I offer myself guidance. My advice is specific and practical. At a networking event, I remind myself that I am friendly and knowledgeable. I focus on smiling and staying updated on the latest industry news. It becomes easier to start conversations with strangers and join in their discussions.

I offer myself affirmation. I notice when I am losing weight or getting along better with my mother-in-law. I celebrate the positive changes I make.

The little things in life are rewarding. I watch a funny movie. Laughter dissolves stress and cheers me up. I prepare my favorite foods. Indulging in a cup of hot chocolate or a kale salad with cranberries restores my energy.

I play with my pets. They remind me that I am loveable.

I spend time with family and friends. They share my victories and setbacks. They support me in everything I do.

I love doing things to lift my spirits. I listen to stimulating music. Housework becomes less tedious when my favorite songs are playing. I exercise regularly. Physical activity fights depression. I head outdoors to surround myself with nature. Flowing water and green fields invigorate me.

Today, I give myself a pat on the back. When I cheer for myself, I am reminded that someone is in my corner. I remember my purpose in life and make positive decisions that support me.

Self-Reflection Questions:

1. How do I know when I need a pep talk?
2. What is one inspiring thing I could say to myself each morning?
3. Why is it important for me to be kind to myself?

I am so happy. My life is meaningful and joyful.

I develop close relationships that are healthy and mutually supportive. I cherish my family and friends. I block out time for my loved ones. I am proactive about scheduling family dinners and weekend outings. I feel understood and cared for.

I make choices that reflect my values. I stand up for my principles.

I slow down. I live mindfully. I focus on the present. I notice the small miracles that happen each day. I savor little pleasures and create beautiful memories.

I balance my work and personal life. I set realistic expectations. I manage my time efficiently. I learn to prioritize and delegate.

I use my strengths and follow my passions. I work on my communication skills and increase my emotional intelligence. I fill my leisure time with rewarding hobbies and activities. I grow vegetables and play musical instruments.

I appreciate nature. I spend time outdoors. I play sports and walk around green spaces. I listen to birds sing and smell the fresh air.

I laugh and play. I share jokes and funny stories. I watch comedies and cat videos. I stage puppet shows with my children and make a game out of household chores.

I help others. I support worthy causes and give back to my community. I volunteer my time and services. I take pleasure in making my neighborhood more vibrant and inclusive.

Today, I am peaceful and content. My world is friendly and warm. My happiness comes from within.

Self-Reflection Questions:

1. What would I tell my childhood self about how to be happy?
2. Is happiness more like a journey or a destination?
3. How does technology affect my happiness?

I am thankful for all opportunities. My attitude reflects my happiness.

I am thankful for all opportunities that come my way. I let go of the idea that things must be ideal for me to be happy. I recognize that every situation has both challenges and rewards.

Basing my sense of wellbeing on the absence of conflict in my life is futile. There will always be challenges, and I cannot delay my happiness because of their presence.

I believe that success comes to those who take action with what they have at hand. Opportunities for small successes often lead to greater possibilities.

For this reason, I choose to look for the opportunities inherent in every circumstance. Even unpleasant situations can lead to better opportunities that would not have been available without facing the challenge.

I know that challenges teach me the patience and other skills I need in order to make the most of my life. Obstacles help develop my character.

I welcome all challenges and I remain open to the good that awaits me with each new opportunity.

By letting go of the expectation of ease or perfection, I enable myself to discover the possibilities within every situation. I create my own happiness, even in the midst of challenges.

Self-Reflection Questions:

1. Am I waiting for perfection in order to be happy?
2. Do I view challenges as obstacles or opportunities?
3. What opportunity has come to me unexpectedly because I remained open to finding the good in a tough situation?

I am true to myself.

I value honesty and authenticity. I live according to my values. I set priorities and stand up for my principles. I make intentional choices that help me to reach my goals. My motivation comes from within.

I cultivate my passions. I spend time doing what I love. I use my strengths and try new things. I continue learning.

I trust my instincts. I listen to my inner voice and embrace my emotions.

I communicate tactfully and openly. I speak up at business meetings and family gatherings. I advocate for my needs. I listen to others and show them the same consideration.

I set reasonable boundaries. I let others know how I expect to be treated and the consequences for exceeding my limits.

I create genuine relationships. I share my thoughts and feelings. I engage in deep conversations. I surround myself with family and friends who give me encouragement and support.

I take care of my mental and physical wellbeing. I set realistic expectations. I choose a healthy lifestyle that helps me to reach my potential.

I explore my spirituality. I reflect and pray. My faith helps me to understand my purpose and gives me a clear sense of direction. I appreciate the value of my life and celebrate my connection with others.

Today, I follow my heart. I know who I am and what I want. I am honest and trustworthy. I feel confident and strong. My life is joyful and fulfilling.

Self-Reflection Questions:

1. How can I increase my self-knowledge and self-awareness?
2. What is one thing I can do to feel more authentic at work?
3. How can I balance being myself and meeting social expectations?

I am worthy of my dreams.

I have big dreams and I expect to achieve these dreams. I have earned the right to expect great things to happen in my life. If I do my part, I know I can achieve my goals and expectations.

I deserve for good things to happen in my life. I am considerate of others and treat everyone with the respect they deserve. I am a loving friend and family member. I have the best interests of others at heart.

I do the work each day necessary to deserve success. I work hard and with focus. I am clear on what I desire and do the work required to make my dreams a reality.

I have big goals and expectations that are congruent with my abilities.

I review my goals regularly and allow myself to get excited at the prospect of achieving them. I have detailed goals and plans to make them happen.

I am deserving. My strengths and skills are sufficient to achieve my dreams. I am motivated and capable. I am worthy of my dreams.

Today, I remind myself of why my dreams are appropriate for the person I am becoming each day. I have the confidence needed to be successful in the pursuit of my goals.

Self-Reflection Questions:

1. What are my biggest goals and my plans to achieve them?
2. Am I willing to do the work required to be successful in achieving my goals?
3. What steps do I take each day to make my dreams a reality?

I avoid negative people and situations.

I carefully choose the people I allow into my life. I am in control of my life, and one way I exercise control is by being selective of the people I allow to be part of it.

I know that some people have the ability to create drama and drain my resources. I avoid these people so that I can have an enjoyable life. Negative people are unwelcome in my life.

I also do my best to avoid negative situations. The things that happen in my life are sometimes outside of my control, but I reject negative situations. I avoid situations that make my life more challenging unnecessarily.

I actively remove negative people and situations whenever possible.

I maintain high standards in my life. I am willing to let go of the people and situations that fail to serve me or support my dreams.

I am a positive person, and I love to be around others who are positive.

When I avoid the negative, I find that there are positive people all around me. I can always find a new positive person to bring into my life. My life is full of positive people, but I am always open to adding more.

I love the energy and joy that positive people bring with them.

Today, I reject the negative and embrace the positive. I attract positive people and situations into my life. I am living my life in a positive way and with a positive perspective.

Self-Reflection Questions:

1. What are the negative situations in my life? Why are these situations in my life?

2. Who are the negative people in my life? Why are they part of my life?

3. What can I do to avoid negative people and situations?

_____
_____
_____
_____
_____
_____
_____
_____
_____
_____
_____
_____
_____
_____
_____
_____
_____
_____
_____
_____

I choose to smile and enjoy life to the fullest.

I can choose to be miserable, or I can choose to be happy: I choose to be happy. Happiness is a choice that I make each day. I choose to smile and to see the good in my life. I choose to see the good in the world.

I can choose to be bored, or I can choose to be enthusiastic: I choose to be enthusiastic about life. There are so many interesting things I can do, see, and learn.

I look forward to having an interesting day and experiencing something new. I am fascinated by everything the world has to offer.

I can be pessimistic, or I can be optimistic: I choose to be optimistic. I choose to smile at the possibilities each day has to offer. I expect something great to happen each day. I choose to live my life to the fullest.

I keep my eyes open for something to smile about. I easily find things to smile about several times throughout the day. The world is a magical place to me.

Today, I am smiling a big smile. I am enjoying my life at the highest level and helping others to do the same. Today is going to be a great day, and I am going to enjoy every minute of it.

Self-Reflection Questions:

1. What is something I could do regularly that would allow me to enjoy my life more?
2. What do I dread about each day? What changes can I make to make my life more pleasing to me?
3. What are the things that make me smile? Who are the people that make me smile?

_____
_____
_____
_____
_____
_____
_____
_____
_____
_____
_____
_____
_____
_____
_____
_____
_____
_____

I find my own truth.

I come to the place in my life where it is time for me to find my own truth. I have taken all the classes. I have followed many gurus. Now is the time for me to discover what is true for me.

I realize that my truth may be different than the truth of others. That is okay. I am fine with each of us developing what is true for ourselves.

I am ready to stand up for what is true for me. With so much information swirling around in our world today, it is vital that I stand in my power and truth.

I avoid living my life from a surface perspective. I am taking a deep dive within and adventuring into the depths of my soul to find my truth.

As I explore the deep caverns of my soul, I find nuggets of truth. I know it is true for me because I light up inside. I get giddy. I come alive.

I store these new nuggets of truth in my knapsack for safe keeping. I bring them safely to the surface and share them with others.

I create safe spaces of open communication where all are welcome. Those who have different truths are welcome to share their truths in a safe place of open conversation.

I set ground rules of kindness and appreciation.

I respect other people's opinions and they gladly respect mine. With mutual respect, I find that together we can come up with great solutions.

Today, I am grateful that I have the courage and conviction to stand up for my truth.

Self-Reflection Questions:

1. How can I stand in my truth more fully?
2. What can I do to create safe havens where dialogue is respected?
3. Who do I know that shares my philosophy of truth?

I feel safe and loved.

My world is friendly and secure.

I appreciate myself as I am. I treat myself with compassion. I practice self-care. I eat healthy and exercise regularly. I speak to myself with kind and encouraging words. I remember that I am worthy of love and respect.

I develop mutually supportive relationships. I spend time with family and friends who give me constructive feedback and motivate me to pursue my goals. I enjoy deep conversations and fun nights out.

I maintain reasonable boundaries. I communicate tactfully and directly. I advocate for my needs. I let others know how I want to be treated.

I give generously. I share my time and resources. Helping others makes me feel competent and connected.

I embrace change. I recognize that transitions are a natural part of life. I keep my skills up to date. I welcome new opportunities with enthusiasm. I focus on what I have to gain.

I face reality. Trying to avoid conflicts and challenges can make me more anxious. I deal with situations head on. I give myself credit for trying. I teach myself that I am strong enough to handle what comes my way.

I count my blessings. I pay attention to the times when others reward my trust and shower me with kindness.

I reflect on my life and pray in gratitude. I feel part of something bigger than myself.

Today, I protect myself by making smart choices and turning to my loved ones when I need help. I am supported and safe.

Self-Reflection Questions:

1. How can establishing daily routines help me to feel more secure?
2. What does emotional safety mean to me?
3. How do I express my love?

I embrace growth.

I become stronger and wiser each day.

I make my wellbeing a top priority. I build a solid foundation for my personal development by taking care of my mental and physical health. I watch what I eat. I exercise regularly. I manage daily stress and sleep well at night.

I continue learning. I use my library card. I read books, watch videos, and listen to podcasts. I take courses online or at my local community college. I talk with friends and coworkers about their hobbies and interests.

I connect with others. I cultivate mutually supportive relationships. I share constructive feedback. I engage in deep discussions and listen carefully to different points of view.

I give generously. Practicing random acts of kindness increases my capacity for love.

I advance my career. I study thought leaders and high performers. I adapt their habits to suit my own style. I work on my communication and writing skills. I manage my time and maintain balance.

I seek out inspiration. I spend time outdoors. Natural beauty energizes me and stimulates my creativity. I practice my faith. Prayer and reflection encourage my self-awareness. My life feels more joyful and meaningful.

I celebrate the power of positivity. I believe in myself and my abilities. I learn from experience. I give myself sincere compliments and invigorating pep talks.

Today, I am like a garden in full bloom. I flourish and thrive. I grow my talents with dedication, hard work, and perseverance.

Self-Reflection Questions:

1. Why is personal development a lifelong process?
2. What is my personal mission statement?
3. How do challenges help me to grow?

I flourish despite external circumstances.

I am grateful for the skills and aptitude to think outside of the box. I am grateful for my creative mind. These traits help me to sidestep or overcome any obstacles, even during challenging times when things look grim.

I live life on my own terms regardless of what is going on in society around me. I am grateful that I have been able to avoid the drama.

I am proud of myself for seeing the truth.

I have replaced fear with faith. I am proud of myself each time I can catch my mind before falling into an old fear-based belief. I can see my progress. I give myself an A+.

I am reminded of the adage, "Necessity is the mother of invention." I am free from the pull of guilt and shame. I have overcome my codependent behavior.

Now that I am free to be me, my mind is coming up with all kinds of ideas. I am solution oriented. I think outside of the box. I color outside the lines. I come up with unusual solutions that work!

I refuse to allow others to pull my strings. I have cut my strings. I now know what Pinocchio felt like when he had no strings. I am free from being manipulated by others.

I see now that the whole world is my oyster. I can do anything. I feel my heart swell with gratitude and happiness. I feel my backbone straightening up. I feel my feet planted solidly under me.

Today, I stand my ground. I speak up for myself. I am unafraid. I am FREE!

Self-Reflection Questions:

1. What do I want to do now that I am free?
2. How can I flourish to an even greater extent?
3. Now that I am limitless, what is my next leap of faith?

I forgive myself for all of my past mistakes.

I might be imperfect, but I am still amazing. I am free of the need to be perfect. I am comfortable with making mistakes

I make mistakes because I am brave and willing to try new things. I am committed to living my life to the fullest and that means that mistakes are made.

All humans make mistakes, and I am a human. I avoid expecting myself to be anything other than human.

I learn from my mistakes and put the information I learn to good use. In this way, I can see that mistakes can be helpful.

Whether a mistake is helpful or unhelpful, I forgive myself for it. I let go of all of my mistakes with ease.

I release myself from any guilt, shame, or embarrassment related to my previous mistakes. I am free from any negative feelings related to any mistake I have ever made.

I forgive myself for my future mistakes, too. I have already forgiven myself for these mistakes. I forgive myself for all past, present, and future mistakes.

Today, I am doing my best to avoid making any silly mistakes. However, it is okay if I do make mistakes. I can forgive myself quickly and move on with my day. I am acting bravely today without any fear of the mistakes I might make.

Self-Reflection Questions:

1. What has happened in the past that I need to forgive myself for? Why haven't I forgiven myself yet?

2. What would my life look like if I forgave myself for every mistake I have made?

3. Do I forgive others easily? Would I forgive myself more easily if I regularly forgave others?

I have the power to create my best life.

I believe in myself. I am the master of my own life.

I create the best life I possibly can. I do my best each day. I maintain a positive attitude that brings me the power to create a life that makes me happy.

I believe that knowledge brings me more power, so I continue learning.

I am amazed about the vastness of all knowledge as I realize that it is endless. I am always on the path towards infinite understanding.

I can step back from the world to create my own reality. I can catch myself before getting pulled into the chaos around me. I am thankful for that wisdom.

I realize that the less I plug into the world, the more powerful I become.

I can feel my personal power growing as I choose what is best for me.

I am grateful that I have a lifestyle that allows me the privilege to be in the world but not of it.

I am so happy that I can live my life outside of the mind trips that many people experience. I am extremely grateful that I can see through the confusion.

Today, I know who I am, what I want, and what is right for me. I am building up my inner strength to follow what is true for me in spite of what is going on out in the external world. I have the power to create my best life.

Self-Reflection Questions:

1. How can I stay in a place of solitude in spite of world politics?
2. How can I be a neutral observer?
3. What practices would I like to adopt to strengthen my inner power?

I love and respect myself.

The love I have for myself is the most important love of all. When I love myself, I am better able to love and care for others. I am better to myself and the world when I am able to love myself.

I have great respect for myself and my many accomplishments. Self-respect is an important component of happiness and fulfillment.

I treat myself with the respect I deserve. I am worthy of self-respect and enjoy feeling good about myself. I maintain high standards for my behavior and face the world in a way that allows me to sleep peacefully at night.

My friends and family are proud to be part of my life. It is easy for me to show them love and respect because I maintain these qualities for myself as well.

Self-love and self-respect make it possible to have authentic relationships with others. By accepting and loving myself, I am able to give the same gift to others.

Much of my self-respect come from the willingness to accept responsibility for my own life. The respect I feel for myself springs from this place. I am able to avoid worrying about the negative opinions of others, because I am in control of my life and emotions.

Today, I appreciate my unique qualities. I remind myself how wonderful I am and that I deserve love and respect from the world, but most of all from myself.

Self-Reflection Questions:

1. What are my five greatest qualities? How do these qualities enhance my life and the lives of others?
2. When do I fail to show respect and love to myself? Why?
3. In what ways can I be more respectful and loving to myself?

_____
_____
_____
_____
_____
_____
_____
_____
_____
_____
_____
_____
_____
_____
_____
_____
_____
_____
_____

Letting go is joyful.

I make peace with the past. Instead of dwelling on regrets, I am grateful and content with each experience that helps to make me who I am today. I live in the present moment.

I practice forgiveness. When I pardon others, I unburden myself.

I challenge self-limiting beliefs. I review my accomplishments and take on new challenges. I build my confidence.

I accept that some things are outside of my control. I devote my efforts and energy to activities where I can see results. I work on changing myself, rather than losing sleep over what others are doing.

I cut down on possessions. I sort through junk drawers and closets. I give away items I seldom use. I spend less time cleaning and maintaining things. I make my home more spacious and less stressful.

I shorten my to do list. I free up time for having fun and hanging out with family and friends.

I say goodbye to relationships and situations that no longer serve my needs. I seek friends and partners who appreciate me as I am and share my values. I find a new job that allows me to take on more responsibility or enjoy greater balance.

Today, I free myself from attitudes and habits that hold me back. I let go and move on.

Self-Reflection Questions:

1. What is the difference between giving up and letting go?
2. What is one thing I can do to simplify my life?
3. Why is quality more important than quantity?

My feelings are valid.

I love and accept myself.

I stay calm. I distinguish between myself and what I am feeling. I give myself time to sort things out when I am overwhelmed. I take a walk around on the block or sleep on it.

I am honest with myself. I examine my personal biases and blind spots. I acknowledge my intentions.

I put my feelings into words. I tell myself that it is okay to be sad or angry. I write in a journal or call a friend who I can count on for constructive feedback. Expressing my feelings helps me to understand them and put them in perspective.

I learn how to encourage and motivate myself. I enjoy praise from others, but it is more important that I approve of myself. My confidence is strong and stable.

I increase my self-awareness. When I have feelings that are conflicted or unexpected, I search for the reasons behind them.

I live consciously. I read about psychology and personal development.

I make sound decisions. I listen to my head and my heart. I balance logic and emotion. I take responsibility for my behavior.

I give myself credit for making an effort. Each time I try to validate myself or others, I become more skillful. I focus on progress rather than perfection.

Today, I treat myself with kindness and understanding. I manage strong emotions by accepting them and making wise choices that help me to be happy and successful.

Self-Reflection Questions:

1. What is the difference between justifying my experiences and validating them?
2. How does anger affect my ability to make wise decisions?
3. How does validating others strengthen my relationships?

My confidence is unshakeable.

I believe in myself and my abilities. I think positive. I remember that hard times are temporary, and I control how I react to external circumstances. I look for ways to use any situation to my advantage. I am creative and flexible.

I focus on my strengths and achievements. I take pride in my accomplishments.

I stand tall. Looking confident helps me to feel surer of myself. I hold my head up and make eye contact.

I stay calm under pressure. When I feel tense, I take a few deep breaths and stretch my muscles. I slow down, so I can think clearly and review my options. I relax with a warm bath or a cup of tea.

I advocate for my needs. I stand up for my principles.

I continue to learn and grow. I enjoy gaining new skills and knowledge that strengthen my professional qualifications and enrich my personal life.

I build a strong network of support. I can count on my family and friends for practical assistance, comfort, and reassurance.

I invest in myself. I love and accept myself as I am. I embrace my feelings and validate my experiences. I look after my physical, mental, and spiritual needs.

I take action. I tackle challenges rather than overanalyzing them. Making an effort and seeing results boosts my faith in myself.

Today, I exude confidence. I rid myself of doubts and fears. I can meet life's challenges and reach my goals.

Self-Reflection Questions:

1. Why is it important to value myself?
2. What is the relationship between confidence and success?
3. What is one area of my life where I want to be more confident?

I open the window of opportunity.

I let the light of new beginnings flow into my space. I fling the curtains of doubt open and receive new inspiration!

I actively avoid closing myself off from opportunity. I open up my heart. I breathe in the new beginnings!

I release old patterns of self-sabotage. I gratefully say goodbye to all the limiting beliefs from my past. I dust off the doubt dirt from my shoes and get ready to polish them for what is next!

I buy new clothes that fit my new look. I reinvent myself. I see myself in a whole new light.

I stand tall in my new suit of clothing. I feel confidence shining through. I put on my happy face. I feel my new "me" starting to expand and shine outward.

I expand my thinking to what is my next best step. I boldly stride forward into my future.

I have unlimited opportunities laid at my feet!

I shine with newfound strength. I polish up my attitude. I create my new look.

Now that I have released all those shabby, old thoughts and beliefs, I feel my energy expand. I feel strong, happy, and confident.

Today, I know I can do anything I put my mind to. I am excited about my future. I feel great things are coming through my open window of opportunity and landing in my lap of happiness!

Self-Reflection Questions:

1. What old, worn-out beliefs do you need to throw out now?
2. What can I do to polish up my new image?
3. How can I reflect my new "Me" both internally and externally?

I love myself unconditionally and accept myself as I am.

Even though I sometimes make mistakes, I am a great person. I love myself unconditionally and accept myself as I am. I make an effort to treat myself with kindness and respect. I deserve it.

I have qualities and talents that make me unique and special – unlike anyone else in the world. I have value.

I deserve to be loved. I love myself and am loved by others. I realize that being perfect is a fantasy. I am good enough as I am to be loved and accepted.

I recognize my strengths and talents and forgive myself for my past mistakes. I acknowledge that I am worthy and deserve all the good things in life. I am wonderful.

I honor my best parts and freely share them with the world.

I allow myself to shine.

I am accepting of others as well as myself. It is only through acceptance that my potential can be fully realized.

I am my own best cheerleader. I welcome the support of others, but I have enough support even when standing alone. I am an awesome person and worthy of great things.

I accept all my faults and shortcomings. I am worthwhile.

Today, I give myself permission to be greater than my insecurities. I love myself totally and completely. I accept myself just the way I am. I am a fine person and deserve a good life.

Self-Reflection Questions:

1. What are some things I love about myself?
2. Do I fully accept myself?
3. How can I better love and accept myself?

My past is behind me.

I am putting my past in the rear-view mirror. What happened in the past is irrelevant today. I am allowing myself to be free of everything in my past.

The past is over and done with. Only the present and the future remain. I avoid giving any meaning to anything that has happened to me before today.

I have learned all the lessons the past has to teach me. Once I have learned from my mistakes, I let them go.

My past has made me stronger and wiser. I am becoming a better version of myself each day. I am looking forward rather than backwards.

I am grateful for my past, but it is over. I put my life on hold when I spend time thinking about the past.

I am excited about my future and choose to put my attention there. I feel like I am a blank slate and can write any future for myself that I desire.

Today, I remind myself that my past is behind me. I am free of its limitations. I refuse to carry the burden of the past one more day. I am looking forward to an exciting future that I am creating each day.

Self-Reflection Questions:

1. In what ways am I allowing my past to dictate my future? What is this costing me?

2. What can I learn from my past that would be useful today? What mistakes have I made that I can avoid making again?

3. What would my life be like if I allowed myself to be free of my past? How would I feel if I were able to accomplish this?

_____
_____
_____
_____
_____
_____
_____
_____
_____
_____
_____
_____
_____
_____
_____
_____
_____
_____

The only person who can defeat me is myself.

I am so powerful and capable. I know that I am the only person that can stand in my way. I am the only obstacle I have. Others are powerless to impede my progress.

I am so committed to my success that other people are too intimidated to even consider getting in my way.

I am clear on my objectives and determined to accomplish them. I am willing to persevere where others quit and go home.

I am good at managing myself. I have control over my thoughts, emotions, and decisions. I am able to take the necessary actions needed to be successful.

I am my best ally. I am my greatest cheerleader and supporter. I am a one-person army.

When others try to sabotage my efforts, I am willing to address the situation politely and assertively. I make it clear that I have no tolerance for interference. I then refocus my efforts and get back to work.

Today, I am reaffirming my commitment to myself and to my success. I am avoiding any opportunities to get in my own way. I am feeling positive about my goals and the steps I need to take to achieve them.

Self-Reflection Questions:

1. How do I sabotage myself? Why do I sabotage myself? What would happen if I stopped doing this to myself?
2. What obstacles do other people present to me? Could these obstacles exist primarily in my mind? What can I do to get past them?
3. What are my greatest strengths? How can I capitalize on my strengths in pursuit of my goals?

_____
_____
_____
_____
_____
_____
_____
_____
_____
_____
_____
_____
_____
_____
_____
_____
_____
_____

15 SELF-DISCOVERY QUESTIONS

To Help You Know Yourself Better

How well do you know yourself? Maybe not as well as you think.

One of the best ways to learn about something is to ask questions. This method is especially convenient in this situation because you don't have to go looking for an expert to answer your questions. You can answer them for yourself.

Why would you want to know more about yourself? There are great benefits, with even greater satisfaction with your life! As often stated, "The truth will set you free."

Use these questions to learn more about yourself and live a more meaningful and happier life:

1. **What are the mistakes I continue to make? Why?** It's surprising how successful you can be without doing anything spectacular, provided you avoid repeating your mistakes.

2. **How do I distract myself?** Knowing how you distract yourself can make you more aware of when you're distracting yourself. You can also take steps to avoid your distractions if you identify them.

3. **What are my goals for the next month?** When you know your goals, you can effectively plan your day and ensure that you're making progress.

4. **What are my goals for the next 10 years?** To know your ten-year goal, you need to think about your life and what you want. To achieve a long-term goal, it's essential to mold your life around it.

5. **What do I like about my life?** Answering this question makes you think about the good things in your life. It also makes you grateful and allows you to attract more of those good things.

6. **What do I dislike about my life?** Knowing what you don't like puts you in a position to consider how to make your life better.

7. **What would I do if I weren't afraid?** You'll learn what it is you really want to do by asking yourself this question.

8. **What are the common characteristics of the last three people I dated?** What is your type? Is that a good type or bad type for you? What do you want to look for in your next partner?

9. **What would I change about my job?** What do you like and dislike about your job? What can you do to make your job better? Do you need to find a new position?

10. **When I was a child, what did I want to do when I grew up?** Have you lost sight of what mattered to you when you were younger? Could your earliest plans still be relevant to your life now?

11. **What activity or subject makes me lose track of time while**

I'm doing it? These are the activities you love to do. If you could turn one of these activities into a career, you may find more enjoyment in your daily life.

12. **If I gave myself advice, what would it be?** Imagine someone just like yourself with the same life. What would you tell them to do? The real trick is getting yourself to follow this advice!

13. **What have I never done, but would love to try?** This is a fantastic way to add a little spice to your life. You eventually regret not trying the things that interested you.

14. **What characteristics do I believe I lack, but would love to have?** Whom do you admire and why? How would your life be different if you had these same characteristics?

15. **What do I worry about?** What are the sources of stress and concern in your life? What does this say about your life and yourself? What can you do to reduce the anxiety in your life?

The more you know about yourself, the better you can manage yourself. **Discovering more about yourself also clarifies how you can bring greater joy and fulfillment into your life.**

If you haven't tried to study yourself, you don't know as much about yourself as you could. Getting to know yourself better can pay big dividends!

ABOUT THE AUTHOR

Bonita A. Benson is the founder and CEO of Life Matters Training & Consulting Services and serves as pastor, where she founded New Vision Ministries. Bonita worked as a clinical social worker for 25 years. Her love for helping and coaching others began more than 15 years ago while she was searching for a fulfilling career path. Since then, she has built a large network of women and entrepreneurs who are seeking success in life and business. She has coached thousands of individuals to develop a strong mental and emotional attitude. Today, she continues to coach, mentor, motivate and inspire others through her own struggles, challenges, and accomplishments. She is a dedicated daughter, mother of two children, grandmother of two and entrepreneur.

www.ingramcontent.com/pod-product-compliance
Lightning Source LLC
Chambersburg PA
CBHW071457070526
44578CB00001B/371